chrisbuczinsky
Bill Buczynsky

Pied Poetry

by
Chris and Bill
Buczinsky

A Child's Voice
Arlington Heights, Illinois

Published by:
A Child's Voice
1107 Hawthorne Street, Suite 2-H
Arlington Heights, IL 60005-1071

Library of Congress Control Number: 2001091852

Buczinsky, Bill
Pied Poetry / by Bill Buczinsky and Christopher John Buczinsky;
illustrated by Christopher John Buczinsky
32 p. : col. ill. ; 29 cm.
Summary: a collection of humorous poems about people, pirates, pipers,
bogeymen, giants and other creatures of cloud and conjury.
ISBN 0-9711931-1-8
1. Children's poetry, American. 2. Children's humor—Juvenile poetry.
3. Humorous poetry, American
[1. American poetry. 2. Humorous poetry.]
I. Buczinsky, Christopher John. II. Title

811/.6—dc21   2001091852

Printed in the United States of America

10 9 8 7 6 5 4 3 2 1

for Mom and Dad

"Oh, day and night! But this is wondrous strange
And therefore, as a stranger, give it welcome."

—*William Shakespeare*

"Whatever it was I lost, whatever I wept for,
Was a wild, gentle thing, the small dark eyes
Loving me in secret.
It is here. At the touch of my hand
The air fills with delicate creatures
From the other world."

—*James Wright*

The Gate

Who is stopping?
Who is knocking?
Who is peeping
Through the piper's gate?

Whisper the password,
Soft as you can bear,
Turn three times,
Then, enter if you dare!

My name is Bill.

And my name is Chris.

This is a book of poetry.

Poetry is a game of make-believe. Some people say make-believe is for little kids. But poetry is for all kinds of kids: little kids, big kids, and grown-up kids too.

To play any game you need the right equipment. To play baseball you need a bat and a ball. To play house you need teacups and saucers. To play Fool-Your-Mom-And-Dad, you need—lots of help.

In poetry we play with words. We play with how they sound and what they mean. The first and most important rule of the game is to enjoy yourself.

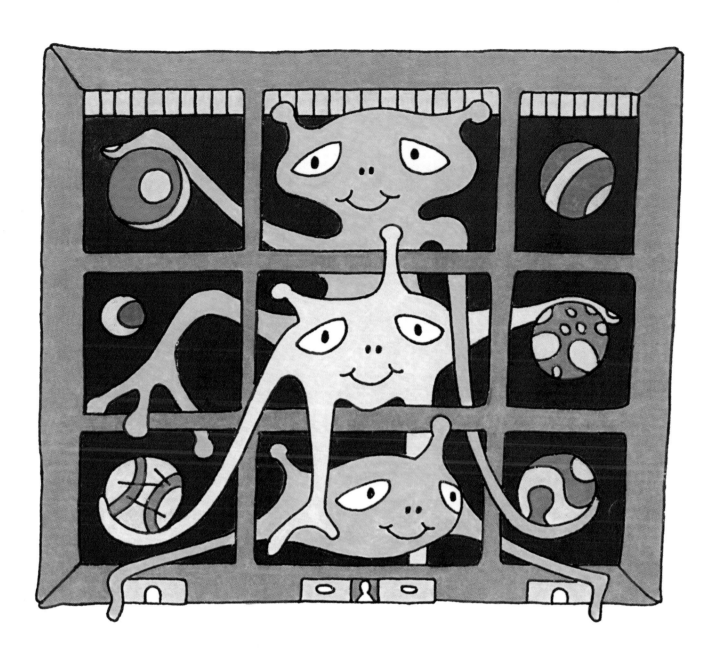

It's also a book of pictures.

Pictures are windows into make believe worlds. The worlds can look just like our world and be peopled with human beings like us, or they can be strange, like planets in outer space and be full of little green aliens.

Pictures are supposed to be pretty. When they're put together right, the lines, shapes, and colors tell you things your head can't know but your heart can't hide.

Just like reading poetry, looking at pictures is a game of make believe. If you make believe hard enough, the creatures inside will come to life. And when that happens, all you have to do is open your window and let them come in.

Something's Shakin'

Something's shakin' up the houses.
Something's turnin' up the ground.
Something's risin' like a rocket.
Something crazy's come to town.

Something big, something tall.
Something I don't understand at all.
Something kool; something kooky.
Something just a little spooky.

Something happy, something sad.
Something good, something bad.
Something nice, something mean.
Something *you've* never seen.

Something's shakin' up the houses.
Something's turnin' up the ground.
Something's risin' like a rocket.
Something crazy's come to town.

The Bogeyman Band

The Bogeyman lives in Bogeyman Land
With his bogeyman friends called the Bogeyman Band.
But on moonless nights when you turn off your lights,
The Bogeyman creeps into your room.
He rattles your windows, slams your door,
Rustles your curtains, slinks 'cross your floor.
You scream, cry, holler, and shout.
You hide under your covers to keep him out.
But he won't go away.
No matter what you say,
No matter what you do,
He plans to stay right there in your bedroom with you.
But there's nothing to fear. Don't start a fight.
Just get out of your bed and turn on the light.
And when you do,
The Bogeyman Band will play its songs for you.
They're wild and crazy, weird as can be.
They're the strangest band you'll ever see.
But the songs they play on their strings
Are the most beautiful songs you'll ever sing.
So don't be afraid, no matter what your friends say.
All the Bogeyman wants to do—is play.

Being Green

They've buttoned me up in a purple coat.
"But I'm green," I say. "I'm green!"

They've snapped,
They've zipped,
They've buttoned me up.
"But I'm green," I say. "I'm green!"

"I'm slippery and sloppy
I'm wet as a frog.
I'm green as the grass," I say.

"I'm meek and mild
I'm wild as a child.
I'm green as the leaves in May."

But they've buckled,
And buttoned,
And shut me up.
"For you're green," they say. "You're green."

The Dog Doctor

I'm the dog doctor.
I fix dogs.
I look in their eyes for motes,
Stare down their long dark throats,
Examine their furry coats,
Then I jot down some notes.

If they're feeling hot,
I give them a shot.
If they're seeing lots of dots,
I tell 'em what they gots.

I check 'em for tics and comb 'em for fleas,
Make sure if you're bit, you don't get rabies.
I tap 'em on their knees, see if they sneeze.
And I check their pee-pee
To see if they have the heebee-geebees.

So, if your dog starts gaggin'
Or his tail stops waggin',
If his chin takes to saggin'
Or his spirit starts flaggin',
Then call me.
I'm the dog doctor.
I fix dogs.

The Pied Pipers

The pipers are piping a playful song.
Grab your baskets and step along.
They're taking us all on a wild goose chase
To a picture perfect place beyond time and space;
Where everyone speaks in rhythm and rhyme.
And everything moves in color and line;
Where there's nothing up your sleeve
But what you make believe,
And there's nothing at all to make you grieve;
Where learning is play, and it's always May—
Except in December, but that's okay
'Cause winter is wonderful anyway.
The pipers are piping a playful song,
Grab your baskets and step along.

Cloud Creatures

Look at the cloud creatures go.
They go so slow.
They go with the flow.

Look at them fly,
Way up high,
Over the trees,
Across the sky,
Just movin' on by.

They have no place to go,
No place to hide.
Some look low.
Some look high.

All day long,
They float along,
With nothing to do
But float on the blue.

I wish I were a cloud creature.
Don't you?

The Irate Pirate

Aye! I'm the Irate Pirate
I shout all day:
"Shiver me timbers.
Get out of me way!"

I'll knock yer block off.
I'll run you through!
Have you walk the plank.
And make shark bait out of you.

I'm rude and reckless.
I shout and scream.
I'm the nastiest sea-dog
You've ever seen.

So you best let me be.
Or I'll cut yer throat.
Leave you on a desert isle
And sink yer boat.

Many a landlubber wants to know why
I'm irate and angry all the time.
Many there be that sail up to me
Asks me to tell 'em why I'm so mean.

I say, "Yo, Ho, Ho!"
Spit in the dirt;
Swallow some rum;
Wipe me mouth on me shirt.

Then I look out to sea
With me one good eye,
Take a long, deep breath
And heave a salty sigh.

You know, it ain't easy sailing the seven seas.
I get sick to me stomach, weak in me knees.
It's hot all day, and at night I freeze.
Why, I've been stranded fer days without a breeze.

Two times tossed in terrible typhoons.
I've been shipwrecked nine times.
And ten times marooned.
I'm chased all day, cursed all night,
So naturally I'm full of fight.

But what's the use complainin'.
You can't understand.
I got a peg for a leg
And a hook for a hand.
I wear a patch on one eye
So I can barely see land.

Land! Aye, and what's there for me?
Me Ma she died when I was just three.
And me Pa was lost in the South China Sea.
So I got no one on land who cares about me.

But I'll sail on in spite of the pain,
Chasin' all the riches in Spain,
Fightin', screamin' and raisin' Cain.

'Cause I'm the Irate Pirate.
I shout all day:
"Shiver me timbers.
Get out of me way!"

Jungle Day

Who wants to sway
In a tropic breeze?
Who wants to swing
From the top of trees?

It's a jungle day.

Who wants to float
Up the River Nile,
Into the jaws
Of a crocodile?

Who wants to jump
Like flames in fire,
Rise like heat
Higher and higher?

It's a jungle day.

Who wants to rattle
A witch's bag,
Battle the brains
Of the Evil Hag?

Who wants to whirl
In a wild trance,
Spin, spit, spurl
In an animal dance?

It's a jungle day.

Shout and scream
In a tribal band:
"Unga-ba Junga-ba"
It's a savage land!

It's a jungle day.

Gentle Giant

Everyone says giants are mean,
But that's not true of the giant we've seen.

The giant we've seen is as big as a mountain.
Niagara Falls is his water fountain!
The Atlantic Ocean barely covers his knees.
And his sneeze makes a hurricane look like a breeze.

Whenever he snores, rain clouds pour,
Rivers rage and valleys roar.
The first time we saw him we wanted to scream.
We thought, "He could snap us in half like a bean!"
But things are not always the same as they seem.

Sure this giant could topple tall towers,
But he'd rather dance in summer sun showers,
Sing silly songs and hum them for hours.
Twinkle his toes in flowery bowers.

He's the funniest giant you ever saw
With a horn for a hat that's strapped to his jaw.
In the middle of June he stares at the moon
'Til his eyes pop out like a crazy goon.

He's sweet as a lamb, cute as a kitten,
Soft as a pillow, warm as a mitten.
We climb up his back, wave from afar,
Jump from his shoulders straight to a star.

But there is *one* thing that scares us all:
It's whenever he gives his dragon a call.
He keeps a dragon named Ganga at home—
Ah, but that's a tale for another poem.

The Slow Poem

The Slow Poem is a slow-poke.
He roams the world real slow.
His rhythm and rhyme take their time.
No need to rush. He's doin' fine.
Too laid-back to race far and near,
He's happy to bring up the rear.
He dallies and dawdles, lingers and lags.
Gets where he's going with a zig and a zag.
You won't see him scramble, scamper, or scurry.
He refuses to hassle with hustle and hurry.

So when you feel like takin' it easy.
When you want life light and breezy—
Go find a Slow Poem.
Take him home.
He'll teach you to smell the flowers,
And turn your minutes into hours.
You'll never again do anything fast
And your mornings, afternoons, and evenings—
Will last and last and last.

Strange World

I just got back from the strangest land
Where to be confused is to understand.
I found everything there terribly confusing.
The most serious people find everything amusing.
Workers work hard by being lazy,
And the sanest people are *really* crazy.
The government enforces the oddest rule:
To become a genius, you must act like a fool.
Beggars are rich and billionaires poor
'Cause nothing valuable is bought in a store.
And the oldest roads lead to the newest places,
Where the oldest souls have the youngest faces.

It really was a mixed-up town,
Topsy-turvy, upside down.
Heaven and Earth were turned around,
So land was sky, and sky was ground.
While visiting there I was lost in space,
My wits had vanished without a trace.
My senses had done a complete about-face.
But when I got home—
I sure missed that place.

The Gate Left Open

For all who pass,
The gate is open.
For all who ask,
The poem is spoken.
The piper plays,
The valleys ring.
Hear the children
Laugh and sing.